HIP-HOP DANCING

DANCING WITH A CREW

VOLUME 4

by Wendy Garofoli

Consultant:
AleKsa "LeX" Chmiel, Co-Director/Owner
Flomotion Dance Company
Philadelphia, Pennsylvania

CAPSTONE PRESS
a capstone imprint

Velocity is published by Capstone Press,
151 Good Counsel Drive, P.O. Box 669, Mankato, Minnesota 56002.
www.capstonepub.com

Library of Congress Cataloging-in-Publication Data
Garofoli, Wendy.
 Hip-hop dancing / by Wendy Garofoli.
   p. cm.
 Includes bibliographical references and index.
 Summary: "Provides step-by-step instructions for learning breaking, popping, locking,
and krumping hip-hop dance moves"—Provided by publisher.
ISBN 978-1-4296-5484-5 (library binding) — ISBN 978-1-4296-5485-2 (library
binding) — ISBN 978-1-4296-5486-9 (library binding) —ISBN 978-1-4296-5487-6
(library binding)
1. Hip-hop dance. I. Title.
GV1796.H57G37 2011
793.3—dc22   2010030394

Editorial Credits

Megan Peterson and Mandy Robbins, editors; Veronica Correia, designer; Marcie Spence,
    media researcher; Laura Manthe, production specialist

Photo Credits

AP Images: Francois Mori, 4–5, Mark Davis/PictureGroup, 27, Phil McCarten/
PictureGroup, 19, Scott Gries/Picture Group, 14, Trae Patton/NBCU Photo Bank, 15;
Capstone Studio: Karon Dubke, cover, 7, 16–17, 30 (left), 31, TJ Thoraldson Digital
Photography, 4, 8–9, 10, 11, 12, 13, 18, 20, 21, 23, 24, 26, 30 (bottom), 32–33, 34–35,
36, 37, 38–39, 40, 41, 44 (bottom), 45; Getty Images Inc.: Michael Caulfield/WireImage,
25; iStockphoto: AleksandarGeorgiev, 22–23 (background), 28–29; Shutterstock: Andrei
Nekrassov, 22 (bottom), bogdan ionescu, 44 (top right), Felix Mizioznikov, 42–43, Gustavo
Miguel Fernandes, 35, Jun Mu, 42, Mark Herreid, 44 (top left), Morgan Lane Photography,
29, Paul-Andre Belle-Isle, 22 (top), skvoor 6.

Printed in the United States of America in Stevens Point, Wisconsin.
092010
005934WZS11

TABLE OF CONTENTS

HIP-HOP CREWS

A hip-hop dancer stands in the cypher with his crew, waiting for his turn to dance. His opponent has just ended his turn with a difficult move that impressed the crowd. The dancer walks into the middle of the circle. He pumps up the crowd with some fast footwork. In a flash, he drops to the floor. Suddenly, the dancer is upside down, spinning on the top of his head. The crowd goes wild. The dancer has just won the battle for his crew.

cypher—a circle that forms around a dancer to give space to dance during a battle

battle—a competition between individual dancers or groups

Winning a battle is exciting for a hip-hop dancer. But being in a crew is about more than winning. It's about working together to improve your dance skills. Hip-hop dance first developed in the 1960s and 1970s. Back then, there were no dance studios where kids could learn the moves. Instead, dancers gathered in groups to practice and invent new steps. These groups called themselves crews.

EARLY CREWS

The first hip-hop dance crews sprung up in New York City and on the West Coast. These early crews came up with many of the hip-hop dance moves seen today. New York crews invented breaking, which features fast footwork and acrobatic stunts. West Coast crews created popping and locking. These dance styles showcase muscle ticks and over-the-top arm movements.

Check out a few of the first hip-hop dance crews:

ROCK STEADY CREW
from: New York City
style: breaking
formed: 1977

ZULU KINGS
from: New York City
style: breaking
formed: mid-1970s

NEW YORK CITY BREAKERS
from: New York City
style: breaking
formed: 1983

THE LOCKERS
from: Los Angeles, California
style: locking
formed: 1973

ELECTRIC BOOGALOOS
from: Fresno and Long Beach, California
style: popping
formed: 1977

Rock Steady Crew

One of the first hip-hop dance crews to hit it big was the Rock Steady Crew. Dancers Jimmy D and Jojo formed this breaking crew in 1977. A couple of years later, Richard "Crazy Legs" Colon joined the crew. He invented popular breaking moves such as the Windmill and the **1990**. Crazy Legs and the Rock Steady Crew started off as a street crew. They battled other crews throughout New York. Eventually, they recorded an album, toured the world, and appeared in the film *Flashdance*. In the movie, Crazy Legs wore a wig and stepped in as lead actress Jennifer Beals' dance double. The crew is still active today, with Crazy Legs as its president. Various branches of the crew perform and teach across the globe.

1990—*a spinning handstand using only one hand*

Today hip-hop dance crews are more popular than ever before. They appear on TV shows and in movies. They compete on stages around the world. With hard work, you can also be a part of an amazing hip-hop dance crew.

GETTING STARTED

Learning the hottest hip-hop dance moves is just one of the perks of dancing in a crew. Members of a crew usually form a close bond. Creative freedom is also a plus when part of a crew. Crews make up their own choreography. They also choose their own music, costumes, and places to perform.

Are you ready to get down with a hip-hop crew? You can create your own crew or join an existing crew. If you'd like to join a crew, following a few simple steps can help.

GET IN TOUCH:

Contact a member of the crew. If the crew has a Web site, it might list an e-mail address or phone number. Ask what it takes to be a part of the crew. The crew member may tell you there are no open spots or inform you of an upcoming **audition**. If you can't get in touch with a member, check the Web site for audition notices.

DRESS TO IMPRESS:

Study the crew's style of dress before you show up to the audition. If they are a breaking crew, wear the right gear to the tryout. If they are known for wearing bright, over-the-top costumes, show up in bright colors!

FACT: Jenn Weber is the director of Decadancetheatre, a Brooklyn-based crew from New York. Weber chooses dancers with passion, unique styles, and easygoing personalities. Weber says getting along with other crew members is just as important as being a skilled dancer.

RESEARCH AND PRACTICE:

Watch the crew you want to join. If the dancers are performing in a battle or a show, go check them out. Study their routines and costumes. Practice hard in the style of the crew before you try out.

choreography—the creation and arrangement of dance steps that make up a routine

audition—a performance by a dancer to see whether he or she is suitable for the crew

STARTING A CREW

If you want to form your own crew, there's a lot you need to know. First, get together with a couple of dancers who want to start the crew with you. Then decide on a dance style, mix of boys and girls, and size for your crew.

DANCE STYLE

Choosing the right hip-hop dance style is the first step in figuring out what kind of crew you want to be. Your crew can focus on one dance style or a mix of styles.

POPPING:
sharp, robotic ticks of the muscles

BREAKING:
fast footwork, floor work, and acrobatic moves

LOCKING:
bold, playful arm movements combined with laid-back footwork

KRUMPING:
highly energetic, often flailing movements that can be improvised

CREW MIX

Will your crew be made up of girls, boys, or a mix of both? It depends on who you feel comfortable dancing with.

JUST THE BOYS:

An all-boy crew usually has more power moves. They often focus on bold, hard-hitting choreography.

CREW SIZE

Once you've chosen the dance style and mix of your crew, it's time to pick a size. Each size has its own pluses and minuses. Here are some things to think about:

SMALL (5-10 DANCERS):

A small crew could result in a close-knit group of dancers. It's easier to plan practices with a smaller group. But a small crew might not be as exciting to watch as a larger group.

MEDIUM (11-20 DANCERS):

With more people, it's harder to schedule practices and performances. But if you can get everyone together for a battle, you will impress audiences and other crews.

GIRLS ONLY:

An all-girl crew could feature hip-hop moves with a feminine flair. They could also impress crowds with powerful tricks and highly stylized choreography.

BOYS AND GIRLS:

A mixed crew gives you a larger pool of moves to choose from. Partner work is another benefit to having a mixed crew. But it also means changing choreography so that it fits both boys and girls.

LARGE (21+ DANCERS):

A big group can sometimes be a big hassle! But it can also mean a big payoff. Imagine if you had a crew of 30 dancers coming up for a battle. The other crews would be shaking in their sneakers!

FINISHING TOUCHES

You've figured out your crew's dance style. You've decided to invite boys, girls, or both into your crew. And you've chosen a size for your crew. Now it's time to add some finishing touches.

NAME: Every crew needs a name. How do you go about finding yours? You could name your crew after your school or hometown. Quest Crew, the season 3 winner of *America's Best Dance Crew (ABDC)*, is named after the dance center where they practice. The name also fit because they were on a quest to be better dancers.

Quest Crew

Ill-Abilities

Luca "Lazylegz" Patuelli formed the Ill-Abilities crew in 2007. The members of this crew have physical disabilities. But they've turned their "limitations" into a unique dance style. For example, a dancer on the crew called Checho was born with a deformity in his legs. His dance style focuses mostly on arm strength. When Checho dances, it looks like he's floating!

Breaksk8

GIMMICK OR THEME: Some crews want to let their dance moves do the talking. But others want to go one step further. A gimmick or theme helps audiences and other crews remember exactly who you are. Choose costumes or uniforms that will help you stand out. For example, the all-male JabbaWockeeZ crew from Los Angeles always performs in masks. And the Midwest crew Breaksk8 performs hip-hop moves in roller skates!

Once you've put the finishing touches on your crew, you're ready to hold basic practices. Work hard to build a solid foundation with your main crew. Wait until you establish your style before opening up the crew to a larger number of dancers.

Chapter 2

PRACTICING WITH A CREW

GEAR UP

Now that you've established your crew, you are almost ready to practice together. But before you crank up the music, you need the right gear. Different types of dancing require different gear.

A BREAKING CREW NEEDS:

- loose clothing for ease of movement
- sneakers with good traction to grip the floor
- kneepads to protect knees during floor work
- helmets or skullcaps to keep hair in place and protect the head during headspins or **freezes**
- wristbands to cushion wrists and elbows during freezes

freeze—*a pause in the middle of a breaking move to add drama*

A POPPING OR LOCKING CREW NEEDS:

- loose clothing for ease of movement
- sneakers or shoes with smooth soles for gliding
- kneepads to protect knees during popping or locking floorwork

Tip

If you'd like to dance as a mixed-style crew, wear lightweight sneakers that offer good support. Make sure they aren't too sticky to glide in.

PRACTICE SPACE

You found your dancers and picked out the right gear. Now it's time to find a practice space. Wherever you decide to practice, make sure it's large enough and that you have permission.

PRACTICE AREAS COULD BE:

- large living room or basement
- garage
- backyard
- park
- dance studio

TIP

Drink plenty of water during practice. Bring a water bottle with you, and take breaks to catch your breath and grab a drink. Bring a healthy snack if you think the practice will last more than two hours.

America's Best Dance Crew

Many dance crews come together specifically for the chance to get on *ABDC*. Hundreds of crews from across the country try out for the TV show. But only 15 crews make it to the finals that are broadcast on TV. Each week, crews face off and perform different hip-hop dance styles. The winner of the show receives $100,000 and the title of "America's Best Dance Crew." Many winning crews have future success.

JabbaWockeeZ—season 1 winner

- filmed Gatorade commercial and a Pepsi Smash performance
- starred in a Las Vegas show called MÜS.I.C.
- toured with The Jonas Brothers and New Kids on the Block

Super Cr3w—season 2 winner

- filmed Pepsi and T-Mobile commercials
- danced on TV show *Lopez Tonight*
- toured the United States

Quest Crew—season 3 winner

- appeared in the movie *Alvin and the Chipmunks: The Squeakquel*
- danced on TV shows *So You Think You Can Dance* and *Dancing with the Stars*
- performed in Snoop Dogg's "I Wanna Rock" music video

We Are Heroes—season 4 winner

- performed on *The Ellen DeGeneres Show* and *The Oprah Winfrey Show*
- appeared in Justin Bieber and Sean Kingston's "Eenie Meenie" music video

JabbaWockeeZ

PRACTICE SCHEDULE

Once you've chosen a practice location, talk to your dancers about a practice schedule. Pick a couple of days per week that work for all or most of your members. Set a light schedule at first, and practice only a couple of hours each week. Add more practice hours as the crew grows and its members become more serious.

Structure crew practices in order to get the most out of your time together. It's easy to goof around with your friends for a couple hours. But if you are serious about your crew, a plan for practice time is a must.

STRETCH IT OUT!

Whether you are practicing hip-hop or ballet, you must begin by stretching your muscles. Set aside a few minutes for crew members to stretch out on their own. You can also create a warm-up for all members to follow. Make sure your stretches and warm-up target all your muscle groups.

NECK AND SHOULDERS:

Tilt your head slowly to the right and left. Tilt your chin upward, and then slowly lower your chin into your chest. Then turn your head to the right and left. Roll your shoulders in circles as well to loosen them up.

QUADRICEPS:

Start in a standing position. Hold onto a wall or piece of furniture for support. Bend your right knee and grab your right foot behind you. Try to touch your right foot to your backside without arching your back. Repeat with your left foot.

SIDES:

Stand with your feet shoulder-width apart. Lean your torso from side to side.

WRISTS:

Roll your wrists in circles. Then sit on the floor and press your hands flat on the ground with your fingers pointed toward you.

HAMSTRINGS:

Sit on the floor with your legs extended straight in front of you. Reach forward to your toes. Point your toes and try to touch your stomach to your legs. Then flex your feet.

HEART:

A fast-moving warm-up, such as jogging in place, will help get your heart pumping and your body ready to dance.

21

THE STEPS

After your warm-up, it's time to work on your dance steps. If there is a crew leader, he or she should come prepared with a few moves for the crew to practice. Other members of the crew should also share their ideas. The more the crew works together, the more everyone will be excited to practice.

Today's Practice Agenda:

✓ 1. Angela will lead the crew in a warm-up.

✓ 2. Monique will teach a new move, the Six-Step.

✓ 3. Jacob will lead the group while we rehearse last week's choreography.

✓ 4. Jacob and Emma will teach new choreography.

You don't have to always practice in the same place. Quest Crew practices in a gym and in a dance studio. They work in the gym when learning difficult acrobatic moves. They practice in the dance studio in front of a mirror to improve choreography.

Focus on certain types of moves for certain practice days. Devote one day to learning toprock moves, which are breaking moves performed standing up. Perhaps another practice could be used for learning popping moves. Focusing each session will give your crew something to look forward to each time you practice.

5, 6, 7, 8

You've practiced with your crew and have a bunch of dance moves down pat. Now it's time to string those moves together to music. Most dancers choreograph to music by breaking down the song into counts of eight. They listen to the rhythm of the song and label each beat as one count. After eight counts are up, they start over at one. A familiar dance phrase is "5, 6, 7, 8!" This is actually a countdown that dancers use to let them know when to begin a routine. After "8," dancers know that the count "1" comes next, which is when they start dancing.

Why do dancers divide songs into counts of eight? Because they use those counts to know when to perform each specific dance step.

For example, count "1" might tell you when to begin a move. The move might finish on count "4." A new move could begin on count "5."

Stage Crews

Some hip-hop dance crews are organized like dance companies. They perform stage shows around the world, entertaining audiences instead of battling other crews. In Philadelphia, a company called Puremovement performs and teaches many styles of hip-hop dance in theaters and workshops. In Los Angeles, the Groovaloos have become a popular popping, locking, and breaking crew. They tour the United States and have even made appearances on *So You Think You Can Dance*. A crew called The Legion of Extraordinary Dancers performed at the 2010 Academy Awards.

The Legion of Extraordinary Dancers

PUTTING THE MOVES TO MUSIC

Once the crew is comfortable with eight counts, it's time to put the moves to music. A few simple steps can help you and your crew create choreography.

Pick a song you'd like to dance to. Listen to its rhythm. Divide the beat of the song into counts of eight.

Think about which steps would look good with the music. Does the song you chose have a fast, energetic beat?

YES

NO

Choose swift-moving breaking and krumping moves.

Choose popping or locking moves that work with a slower beat.

Assign a count for each movement.

Memorize the counts of your steps. Then teach them to the other members of the crew.

When the crew knows the counts, perform them to the song.

All-Girl Crews

Hip-hop dancing was once thought of as a boys' club. Today, many female dancers form all-girl crews that give the boys a run for their money. Los Angeles–based Beat Freaks won first runner-up on *ABDC* season 3. Many of its members tour with artists such as Janet Jackson, Britney Spears, and Missy Elliott. On season 4 of *ABDC*, We Are Heroes become the first all-girl crew to win. Decadancetheatre is a female crew that puts on hip-hop ballets. The crew tours throughout the United States, the United Kingdom, and France. Its members also teach hip-hop dance classes.

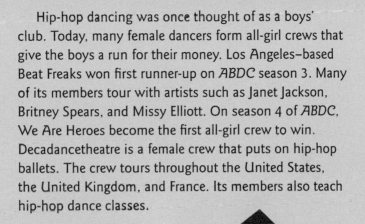

We Are Heroes

Chapter 3

EXPANDING A CREW

Once you've put together a few routines, you might be ready to expand your crew. But finding good crew members can be a tough task. You want talented dancers in your crew. But you also want people who will get along with other members. Some crews require new members to battle every member of the crew to join. Another way to find great dancers is to hold auditions.

WANTED!

New members for

The Dream Crew

AUDITION:

Saturday, April 24 at 12 p.m.
Hip-Hop Dance Mission Studio

Bring sneakers, kneepads, and a dance resume.

For more information call Veronica at 555-8888.

Tip

Members of the Beat Freaks didn't start off as an organized crew. Many of its members were already successful dancers. When they started working together on dance projects, they realized they would make a great all-girl crew.

Before you hold an audition, generate interest in your crew. There are a few ways to let people know you are looking for new members:

WORD OF MOUTH: Tell everyone you know! Spread the word at your school, dance studio, or even family gatherings. Create buzz about your crew by being seen at local events like carnivals, concerts, and festivals.

FLYERS: Create a flyer with the most important information about your audition. Include the time and place of the audition. Also include any moves or gear dancers should come prepared with. Put the flyers up at your school, studio, and on community bulletin boards. Make sure you have permission before you hang your flyers.

ONLINE: Post your audition notice online at Web sites or social networking sites. You could even create your own crew Web site to broadcast your audition.

AUDITION TIME

A well-organized audition lets you make the most out of your time with new dancers. Some simple steps can help you prepare.

Step 1

Use a black marker to write numbers on small pieces of white paper. Have each dancer safety pin a number to their clothes where it can easily be seen.

Step 2

Choose a crew member to teach a small section of choreography, called a combination, to crew hopefuls.

Step 3

Break the dancers up into groups of three or four. Have them perform the combination in those groups.

Step 4

Judges should carefully watch each small-group performance. Judges can be other members of your crew or outsiders, such as dance teachers. Judges should write down notes according to the number pinned on each dancer.

Step 5

Bring a video camera. Auditions go by quickly, so it's best to tape each performance.

Step 6

Save time at the end of the audition for special tricks. Ask dancers to freestyle to the music to get a sense of their personal style.

Step 7

Is choreography important to your crew? If so, ask crew hopefuls to perform their own eight count of choreography.

CALLBACKS

During the audition, you'll probably get a sense of which dancers you'd like to invite into the crew. If you want to see your favorites dance again, hold a second audition, or callback.

When the audition is finished, call out the names of the dancers you'd like to see at the callback. Thank the rest of the dancers for their time. It takes guts to show up to an audition and dance for strangers! You can also call each dancer at home to let them know if they've made it to the callback.

Before you meet with the callback dancers, watch the audition video. It might show you more detail than you remember from the audition. You might also see another dancer you want to invite back whom you didn't notice before.

The callback is about more than just dancing. Get to know the dancers' personalities. Hold one-on-one interviews. Learn about their interests and hobbies. The more you know about the dancers, the easier it will be to choose new members.

At the end of the callback, meet with the other crew members. Decide which dancers to invite into your crew. Finally, announce the names of the newest crew members. Congratulate everyone for a great audition experience.

Collect contact information from everyone at the audition. You'll need it if you want to invite dancers to a callback. You could also invite dancers to future auditions or shows.

You now have a complete crew!

Chapter 4

PERFORMING WITH A CREW

With a complete crew, it's time to find a place to show off your moves. If you hear about an upcoming battle, sign up your crew to compete. Battling other crews is a great way to improve your dance skills. You might even be able to register for local dance competitions under the category of hip-hop group. If you'd rather perform than compete, there are many events to check out.

Is there an upcoming talent show? Sign up your crew to perform.

SPORTS GAMES & PEP RALLIES:
Ask your school if you can perform during halftime at a football or basketball game. Put on a show at the pep rally to raise school spirit.

DANCE STUDIO:
If your crew belongs to a dance studio, perform at their recital.

FESTIVALS:
Many towns hold festivals for different seasons, foods, or even arts and crafts. See if you can get your crew to perform there.

PARADES:

A hip-hop crew would be a huge crowd-pleaser at a local parade. Ask town officials if they'd like to see you dance for them.

FRIENDS AND FAMILY:

When in doubt, perform for friends and family. Put on a show at a barbecue or dinner to knock the socks off those you love.

ONLINE:

If you can't find a live audience, film a routine and post it online. If a lot of people view your video, you'll know your crew is going places!

Online Battle

In 2008 Miley Cyrus held a hip-hop dance battle on YouTube. Miley's crew of dancer friends competed against the director and dancers from the film *Step Up 2*. The battle grew so large that millions of fans clicked on the videos for months. Celebrities such as Channing Tatum, Adam Sandler, and Lindsay Lohan made appearances in the videos.

SYNCHRONIZATION

When getting ready for a battle or performance, you want to make your routine as sharp as possible. One of the best ways to turn an ordinary routine into an unforgettable one is to practice synchronization. How do you get your crew to become synchronized? You run drills.

> **synchronization**—the act of two or more dancers performing the same dance steps at exactly the same time

Not Synchronized

In the army, a drill sergeant makes his troops do something over and over again until they get it perfect. In a crew, it's the same concept.

Synchronized!

Start with an eight count, and have the dancers freeze between each count. The dancers should look around to see where their bodies stopped.

Fix everyone's position so that they look exactly the same. Repeat this process for every count. As the dancers become familiar with their body positions, they can dance all the way through the eight count with the music. Do this for the entire routine!

FORMATIONS

When crew members perform a routine, they usually don't head out on the floor and dance wherever they want to. Instead, they dance in formations.

formation—an arrangement of dancers performing together as a unit

formation example A

Dancers stagger their positions so the audience can see everyone. The space between two dancers is called a window.

formation example B

To make a routine more interesting, have your dancers change formations several times. Choose dance steps that make it easy to move from one formation to another. Don't plan any big tricks while your dancers change formations. Make it easy for dancers to move past one another and stop in a new formation.

formation change example

SPECIAL EFFECTS

Routines are more fun to watch when you add special effects. One way to make a routine stand out is to create a contagion. A contagion works just like singing in a round. Take the popular song "Row, Row, Row Your Boat." People who sing the song break it up into three groups. Everyone sings the same words, but they start singing them at different times.

You can do the same thing in a routine, only with dance steps. Everyone learns the same set of moves, but they start them at different times. This creates a ripple effect that is fun to watch—and even more fun to dance!

contagion—a group of dancers performing the same steps at different times, one after the other

High Level

Middle Level

Low Level

Another way to punch up your routine is to add different **levels**. While some people dance standing up, others should perform similar moves while sitting or lying on the floor. Add a third level by having some dancers kneel or bend at the waist.

level—the height at which a dance move is performed

Crews win points by showcasing individual dancers' tricks. Make room in your routine for dancers to wow the crowd with freezes, flips, or really sharp popping moves.

Freeze

The other crew members can form a half circle and cheer them on. They can also perform simple moves that don't distract from the trick. If you add all these elements to your routine, be prepared for wild applause!

FINISHING TOUCHES

Once your crew finds the right costumes, add even more style with accessories and makeup. Dress up a cool costume with bandanas, hats, wristbands, gloves, and belts. Just make sure you feel comfortable wearing the accessories while you dance.

Makeup can also help dress up a costume. Draw an interesting pattern on your arms or face. Add some glitter to really sparkle!

Tip

Keep budget in mind when choosing costumes, accessories, and makeup. Will crew members need to pitch in their own money to buy the costumes? If so, make your own T-shirts, or put together costumes with clothes you already own.

A SOLID CREW

With great dancers, killer routines, and eye-catching costumes, your crew will be ready to rock. Anyone in a crew will tell you that the friendships made with fellow crew members can last a lifetime. Whether you end up battling or performing together, the most important lesson is to have fun!

GLOSSARY

1990—a spinning handstand using only one hand

audition (aw-DISH-uhn)—a performance by a dancer to see whether he or she is suitable for the crew

battle (BAT-uhl)—a competition between individual dancers or groups; the dancers who receive the loudest crowd applause win

choreography (kor-ee-AH-gruh-fee)—the creation and arrangement of dance steps that make up a routine

contagion (kuhn-TAY-juhn)—a group of dancers performing the same steps at different times, one after the other

cypher (SY-fuhr)—a circle that forms around a dancer to give space to dance during a battle

formation (for-MAY-shun)—an arrangement of dancers performing together as a unit

freestyle (FREE-styl)—to create dance movements on the spot

freeze (FREEZ)—a pause in the middle of a breaking move to add drama

level (LEV-uhl)—the height at which a dance move is performed

synchronization (sing-kruh-nye-ZAY-shun)—the act of two or more dancers performing the same dance steps at exactly the same time

READ MORE

Fishkin, Rebecca Love. *Dance: A Practical Guide to Pursuing the Art.* The Performing Arts. Mankato, Minn.: Compass Point Books, 2011.

Fitzgerald, Tamsin. *Hip-Hop and Urban Dance.* Dance. Chicago, Ill.: Heinemann Library, 2009.

Freese, Joan. *Hip-Hop Dancing.* Dance. Mankato, Minn.: Capstone Press, 2008.

INTERNET SITES

FactHound offers a safe, fun way to find Internet sites related to this book. All of the sites on FactHound have been researched by our staff.

Here's all you do:

Visit *www.facthound.com*

Type in this code: 9781429654876

INDEX